THE MAZE

by Suzanne Stephenson | **Illustrated by** Kraig Jardine

Copyright© 2025 Suzanne Stephenson
The Maze

No part of this publication may be reproduced, distributed, or transmitted in any form or by any means, including photocopying, recording, or electronic or mechanical methods without the prior written permission of the Author, except in the case of brief quotations embodied in the critical reviews and certain other non-commercial use permitted by copyright law.

eBook ISBN: 978-1-965761-84-7
Black and White Paperback ISBN: 978-1-965761-85-4
Color Paperback ISBN: 978-1-965761-87-8
Color Hardcover ISBN: 978-1-965761-86-1

Illustrator: Kraig Jardine
Interior Layout: Marigold 2K
Cover Design: Kraig Jardine

THE MAZE

by Suzanne Stephenson

Dedication

Suzanne Stephenson:

"I dedicate this book to my Heavenly Father. He provided this experience for me when I was a young child and helped me to know without a doubt that He is near me and wants to help me through challenges that can help me come closer to Him throughout my life."

Kraig Jardine:

"Dedicated to my mother, Jeanette Godfrey Esancy."

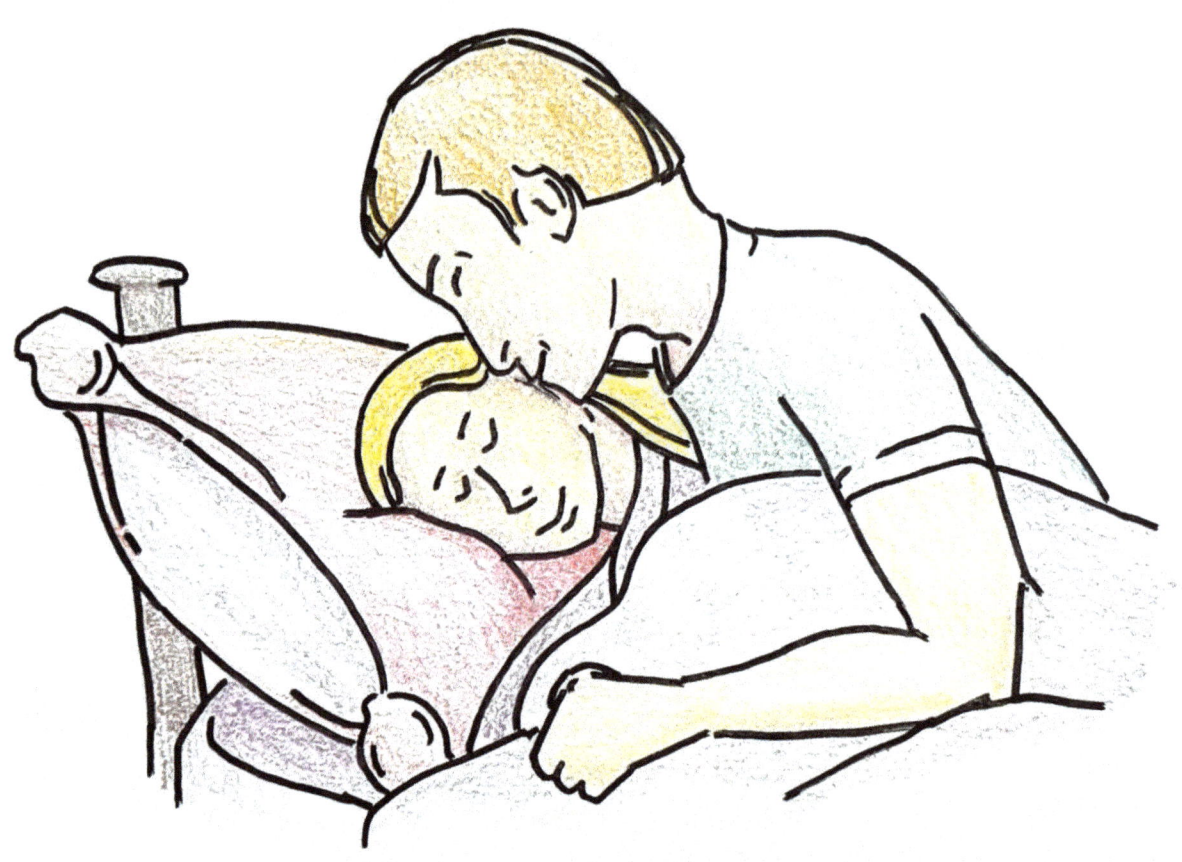

"Sleep well tonight Christine," Dad said as he kissed his daughter goodnight. "Big day tomorrow."

"What time are we moving tomorrow?" Christine asked through a tired yawn.

"The movers will be here at 9:00 in the morning to help us get everything to our new house," Dad replied. "I love you, Sweetheart."

"I love you, too, Dad." Christine rolled over as her dad walked out of her room. Her family had been working hard all week to pack and get everything ready to move to their new home in a different neighborhood.

Christine was excited about the move. A year and a half ago, her family moved from California to Illinois where her father was working as a college professor at the University of Illinois. They had been renting a house in an area where mostly college students lived.

No one Christine's age lived near her, and there was a busy street that separated her family from the neighborhood where her school friends lived. She fell asleep thinking about how fun it would be to have friends to play with that lived close to her.

Christine, Sweetheart, it's time to get up," her mother said softly from her bedroom doorway. "The movers will be here soon."

Christine rolled over, got out of her bed, and stretched with an excited smile on her face. She changed her clothes and put her pajamas, pillow, blanket, and sheets into an open box.

She went to her window and saw the moving van backing into their long driveway. Her mother came into her room, looked around the room and into the closet, and asked, "Did we get everything in here packed?"

"Yes, we did," Christine answered.

"That's great!" her mother said. "Please bring this box out by the driveway," she said as she taped it shut.

As she went to grab the box, Christine looked around the room and under the bed to make sure it was all cleared out. As she looked around, she remembered many good experiences she'd had with her family while living there. She was happy about those memories. She was also happy to be moving to their new home in a neighborhood where she would be going to a different school and making new friends.

She took a breath of excitement, picked up the box, and carried it to the front yard.

The movers were busy loading their furniture and boxes into the moving van. Christine put her box with other boxes by the driveway. "Thank you for bringing the box down," her mother said, giving her a nice hug. They stayed outside, watching the movers work hard, and enjoying the beautiful summer day.

After a while, the movers finished packing the van. Dad was talking with them. He called out to Mom, Christine and her three sisters. "It's almost time to leave. The moving van is packed. Please get into the car. Leon and I will check to make sure all of our stuff is out of the house."

Dad and their older brother, Leon, walked back inside the house, while Mom, Christine and her sisters got into the car.

Not long after they began their drive, they went down a road where there was a field of cattle. The smell of the cows was not pleasant, and Dad, breathing in deeply, said, "Inhale your vitamins!" He enjoyed joking around a bit.

A few minutes later, they entered an area where there were several houses. Leon excitedly told Christine, "Look Christine! There's your new school!"

He pointed out the window. Christine was excited, as well. The playground looked wonderful with swings, slides, basketball hoops, a volleyball net, and soft grass to play on.

She saw some kids out there having fun. "This is going to be so much better than the school we've been going to!" Christine shouted with joy.

When they arrived at their new house, Dad pulled into the driveway, and the moving van parked on the street with the rear door by the driveway. While it was getting emptied and things were being taken into the house, Christine saw three girls her age walking toward her with their bikes from across the street. They were smiling and seemed excited to see her.

"I am Valerie," one of the girls said. "What is your name?"

"I'm Christine," she replied.

"We're excited that you're moving in here," said another girl. "I'm Sarah! I live in that house," she said, pointing to her house just across the street.

The third girl stepped closer to Christine. "I am Linda, and there's my house," she said pointing to the house next-door to Sarah.

Christine was very excited to meet her new friends.

"I am so happy to meet you Valerie, Sarah, and Linda!" she exclaimed, pointing to each one as she said her name.

They continued to talk for a bit. Then Linda asked Christine, "Do you have a bike?"

"Yes, I do," replied Christine.

"Do you want to come with us on a bike ride around the neighborhood now?" Valerie asked.

"I would love to," Christine said. "I'll ask my mom if it's ok." Her mom said she could go on the bike ride with her new friends. Christine grabbed her bike and returned to the girls.

Sarah began to tell Christine about their bike ride. "We call this ride 'the MAZE.' We go through the neighborhood turning left or right at some of the corners. Sometimes we go straight through when roads cross. Our goal is to make it back here," she said, pointing down at the street where they stood. "It can be a bit tricky, especially since you are new in this neighborhood. So, just follow us through. We've done it enough times that we know where to turn. Let's do it!"

They all got on their bikes and rode down the street together. Christine stayed behind Sarah and Valerie, who led the way. Linda rode beside Christine through the neighborhood, and they enjoyed talking while they rode.

The first road they turned onto was right next to a cornfield. It was beautiful, and it smelled so good!

Christine loved the fact that her family was living in a neighborhood that was surrounded by farmland.

They continued to ride through the neighborhood for about half an hour, turning right and left and going straight. Christine enjoyed being with her friends.

Suddenly, Sarah and Valerie stopped at a corner with a stop sign. As Christine stopped behind them, she saw the cornfield she had seen at the beginning of their ride in front of them. She loved watching birds fly over the field. The girls looked both ways, then turned right and headed back to their street.

After arriving back in the area of their homes, they got off their bikes and talked a bit longer before going home. Christine excitedly thanked the girls for being so kind and friendly to her. Valerie said, "We'll definitely go on more bike rides together!" They each went to their own houses. Valerie walked to the house that was next-door to Christine's.

A couple of days later, Christine was taking trash bags out to their garbage bin after she and her family had worked most of the day emptying boxes and putting things away. The day was beautiful! The air smelled wonderful! She thought, "I need to go on a bike ride!"

She hurried into the house and told her mom that she was going to go for a ride. After getting her bike from the garage, Christine looked around to see if any of her friends were outside. She wanted to ride through the maze again. She didn't see any of them. "Hmmm," she thought. "Let's see if I can do this myself."

She got onto her bike and rode down her street until she came to the street that was next to the cornfield. She turned left onto that street and enjoyed looking out over the field, like she had the first time she rode with her friends.

When she realized that the sun was getting close to sunset, she thought she ought to hurry and get through the maze. She turned left onto a street with houses on both sides. She rode until she came to an intersection. She turned right and kept riding. She made several turns along the way.

Suddenly, she stopped and looked around. She did not know where she was. While she had been riding around with her friends, she had mostly just followed them without paying much attention to where they were turning, and without looking for landmarks that she would recognize later on.

Looking around her and not knowing which way to turn, and seeing that the sun was getting lower in the sky, Christine began to panic. She needed to get home safely. And she knew her mother would be very worried if she did not get home before dark. She looked around again, not knowing which way to turn.

As her fear grew stronger, a thought came to her mind: "Heavenly Father knows where you are. He knows where your home is. Pray and ask Him to guide you home."

Christine took a deep breath and, standing next to her bike, bowed her head, closed her eyes, and said a prayer in her mind: "Dear Heavenly Father. I know Thou knows where I am. I know Thou knows where my house is. I don't want my mother to be afraid because I am not home before dark. Please guide me and help me get home safely. In the name of Jesus Christ, Amen."

Opening her eyes, she got on her bike and began to ride, not knowing immediately which way to go. She continued to ride, turning right when the thought came to turn right, and turning left when she felt she should turn left.

Suddenly, she came to a T in the road. Looking to see which way she should turn, she recognized the cornfield she had seen and enjoyed before, and she knew then which way to turn to get home. As she completed her ride back to her house, she knew and was grateful that the Holy Ghost had actually spoken to her, telling her to speak to Heavenly Father and ask for His help. He heard her prayer and showed her the way home.

As she turned onto her street, the sun was close to going down. She rode quickly to her house, put her bike into the garage, and went into her house. When she saw her mother in the kitchen, she went and gave her a hug. Her mother asked, "How was your bike ride, Christine?"

Thinking about Heavenly Father's guidance in her fearful moment, Christine replied, "It was wonderful, Mom!"

"I'm glad you enjoyed it, and that you got home safely, Christine," Mom said.

"Me too!" Christine said with a grateful smile.

About Suzanne Stephenson

Suzanne Stephenson is a former English and Reading teacher and the mother of six children. She has spent many years serving in her church, where her greatest joy has been teaching children.

The Maze is drawn from a formative experience in her own childhood that taught her the power of prayer and the love of a caring Heavenly Father.

About Kraig Jardine

Kraig Jardine grew up with a pencil in his hand and a head full of pictures. Encouraged by dedicated teachers and opportunities to paint from life, he discovered early the joy of creating art that speaks to the heart. Working today as a plein-air painter and illustrator, Kraig is inspired by the quiet beauty of Utah's landscapes and the excitement of bringing stories to life through images. When he isn't painting outdoors, he can be found spending time with his family in Brigham City, Utah, where he continues to pursue the belief that real art never grows old – it speaks to you every time you see it.

www.ingramcontent.com/pod-product-compliance
Lightning Source LLC
Chambersburg PA
CBHW061349010526
44107CB00011B/879